SHAPES

Crescents

by Julia Vogel
illustrated by Sharon Holm

Content Consultant: Paula J. Maida, Ph.D.
Department of Mathematics, Western Connecticut State University

red
wagon

visit us at
www.abdopublishing.com

Published by Red Wagon, a division of the ABDO Publishing Group, 8000 West 78th Street, Edina, Minnesota, 55439. Copyright © 2008 by Abdo Consulting Group, Inc. International copyrights reserved in all countries. All rights reserved. No part of this book may be reproduced in any form without written permission from the publisher. Looking Glass Library™ is a trademark and logo of Red Wagon.

Printed in the United States.

Text by Julia Vogel
Illustrations by Sharon Holm
Edited by Patricia Stockland
Interior layout and design by Becky Daum
Cover design by Becky Daum

Library of Congress Cataloging-in-Publication Data

Vogel, Julia.
  Crescents / Julia Vogel ; illustrated by Sharon Holm.
      p. cm. — (Shapes)
  ISBN 978-1-60270-044-4
1. Curves—Juvenile literature. 2. Geometry, Plane—Juvenile literature. 3. Shapes—Juvenile literature. I. Holm, Sharon Lane, ill. II. Title.
QA483.V62 2008
516'.152—dc22
                        2007004720

Crescents are like moons, you know.

Spy one everywhere you go.

Two rounded arcs that curve and meet

in two small points, sharp and neat.

5

Crescents hide, so can you look?

Can you find them in this book?

6

Spot a crescent in the sky.

See the shape in the pie.

Choose a crescent you can eat.

Pick a crescent that tastes sweet.

Wear a crescent in your hat.

Find a crescent on the mat.

Hang a crescent on a tree.

Hang a crescent letter *c*.

AKES

15

Use a crescent you can rock.

Spot a crescent near the crock.

Draw a yellow crescent moon.

Scoop a crescent with a spoon.

Make a crescent on your face.

Take a crescent everyplace!

With crescents hiding all around,

how many crescents have you found?

I Spy a Crescent Game

Look around. Find a crescent. Then say: "I spy a crescent that is…" and name its color. Everyone has to guess what crescent you see. Then it is someone else's turn to spy a crescent. You can guess what it is.

Count the Crescents Game

Pick a room in your home. Count how many crescents you can find.

Words to Know

arc: the curved part of a circle or a curved line.

crescent: a curved shape, inside and out, like the moon in its first or fourth quarters.

crock: a jar or pot.

shape: the form or look something has.